The Earth Book

by Mic Fox

ISBN 9781692152536

For Roscoe and Dewey,

May you be brave and creative
in difficult times.

May you bring goodness to this world
and peace to those around you.

It may be dry
and hot

The heat may
bring you pain

But one day the
clouds will come

Because you
cannot stop
the rain

It may rain
for weeks and
weeks

It seems the
sky is on
the run

But one day
the sky will
clear

Because you
can't undo
the sun.

The sun will
bring more heat

As your garden
slowly dies

But soon enough
the Moon
will come

And the moon
will change
the tides

And the tides
may bring more
rain

And the wind
may quickly
shift.

We must
protect
our
mother.

For our
time
here

is a
gift.

You can believe what ever you choose
but that doesn't change the facts.

The fact is, we must change.

The world keeps turning —
with us or without us

www.ingramcontent.com/pod-product-compliance
Lightning Source LLC
Chambersburg PA
CBHW040053240726
48664CB00004B/1167